monday morning®

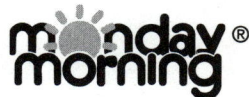

Storybook Patterns

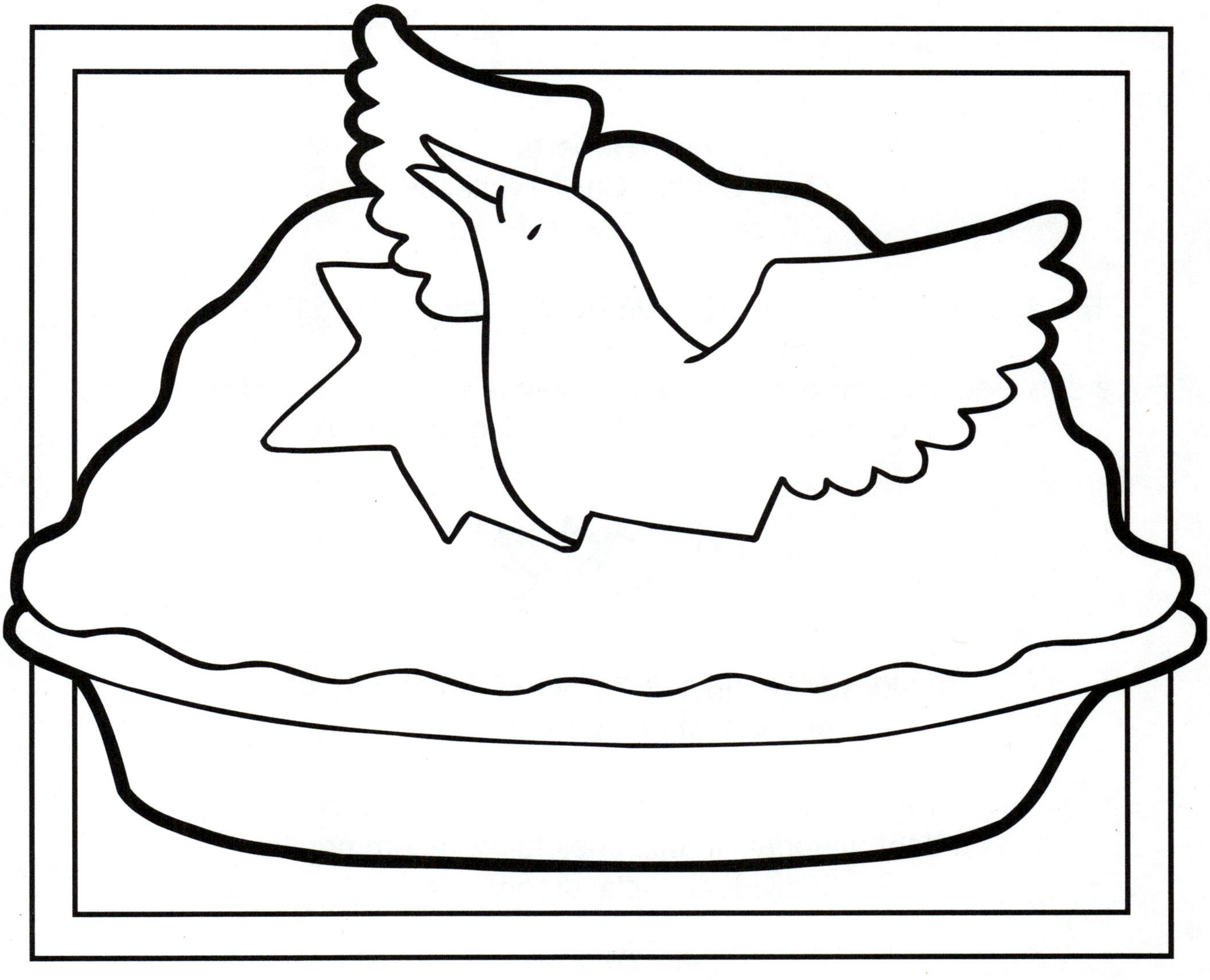

written and illustrated by
Marilynn G. Barr

Publisher: Roberta Suid
Copy Editor: Carol Whiteley
Production: MGB Press

Entire contents copyright © 1995 by Monday Morning Books, Inc.

For a complete catalog of our products, please write to the address below:
P.O. Box 1680, Palo Alto, California 94302

Monday Morning is a registered trademark of
Monday Morning Books, Inc.

Permission is hereby granted to reproduce
student materials in this book for non-commercial
individual or classroom use.

1-878279-81-5

Printed in the United States of America

987654321

Table of Contents

Introduction 4
Alice in Wonderland 5
The Mad Hatter 6
Beauty 7
The Beast 8
Cinderella 9
The Fairy Godmother 10
The Prince 11
The Donkey Prince 12
The Wizard 13
The Emperor 14
The Emperor 15
The Magic Fish 16
The Poor Fisherman 17
The Gingerbread Man 18
Humpty Dumpty 19
The King's Horses and the King's Men 20
The Itsy Bitsy Spider 21
Jack and His Beanstalk 22
The Giant 23
Old King Cole 24
A King 25
The Little Mermaid 26
Three Pairs of Mittens 27
Three Little Kittens 28
Peter Pan 29
The "Clock-odile" 30
Captain Hook 31
An Old Lady 32
The Princess and the Pea 33
The Queen of Hearts 34
A Queen on a Throne 35
Rapunzel 36
A Blackbird Pie 37
A Maid 38
Thumbelina 39
Thumbelina and the Fairy Prince 40
The Ugly Duckling 41
The Swan 42
Rip Van Winkle 43
A Princess 44
A Flock of Wild Swans 45
A Fox 46
Yetta 47
A Zebra in a Zoo 48

Introduction

Storybook Patterns contains 44 patterns for more than 20 different fairy tales. The patterns can be used as storytelling tools, as decorative displays, for creative play, and for skills practice craft activities. Encourage children to make up stories or retell stories in their own words.

Big Books
Prepare poster board pages for each story. Use crayons or markers to decorate the border of each page. Color and cut out patterns for each story and mount them on the poster board. Write the matching story on a construction paper shape. Glue the story onto the page and add a title.

Shape Folders
Provide children with patterns to color and cut out. Glue each pattern to the front of a construction paper or oak tag folder. Then cut around the pattern to form a shape folder. Do not cut along the fold. Position narrow patterns further away from the folded edge.

Glittering Storybook Pictures
Reproduce patterns for children to cut out and glue onto a sheet of poster board. Provide children with markers, glue, brushes, and colored glitter. Show children how to color and/or paint with glue one area at a time. Then sprinkle on colored glitter.

Placemats
Provide 12" x 18" sheets of construction paper and the patterns in this book for students to make fairy tale placemats. Children can use crayons or markers to draw a decorative border around their mats. Laminate placemats before use.

Puzzles
Color and cut out two identical patterns. Glue one pattern to a manila envelope. Write a title on the envelope. Glue the second pattern on to a 9" x 12" sheet of oak tag or construction paper. Cut the picture into four simple puzzle pieces. Laminate the envelope and picture. Store puzzle pieces in the envelope.

Storybook-land Bulletin Board
Reproduce, color, and cut out the patterns in this book. On your bulletin board mount an outdoor scene including, hills, bushes, trees, and clouds. Display story book scenes and handwritten titles on the board for children to enjoy.

Scene Puppets
Some patterns contain a variety of elements found in individual stories. Have each child color, cut out, and glue a pattern to a sheet of oak tag. Help each child trim excess oak tag. Provide children with paint stirrers to glue to the backs of patterns. Have children display puppet scenes as you read or as a child retells a story.

Alice in Wonderland

© 1995 Monday Morning Books, Inc.

The Mad Hatter

Beauty

© 1995 Monday Morning Books, Inc.

7

The Beast

Cinderella

© 1995 Monday Morning Books, Inc.

The Fairy Godmother

© 1995 Monday Morning Books, Inc.

The Prince

The Donkey Prince

The Wizard

The Emperor

The Emperor

The Magic Fish

The Poor Fisherman

© 1995 Monday Morning Books, Inc.

The Gingerbread Man

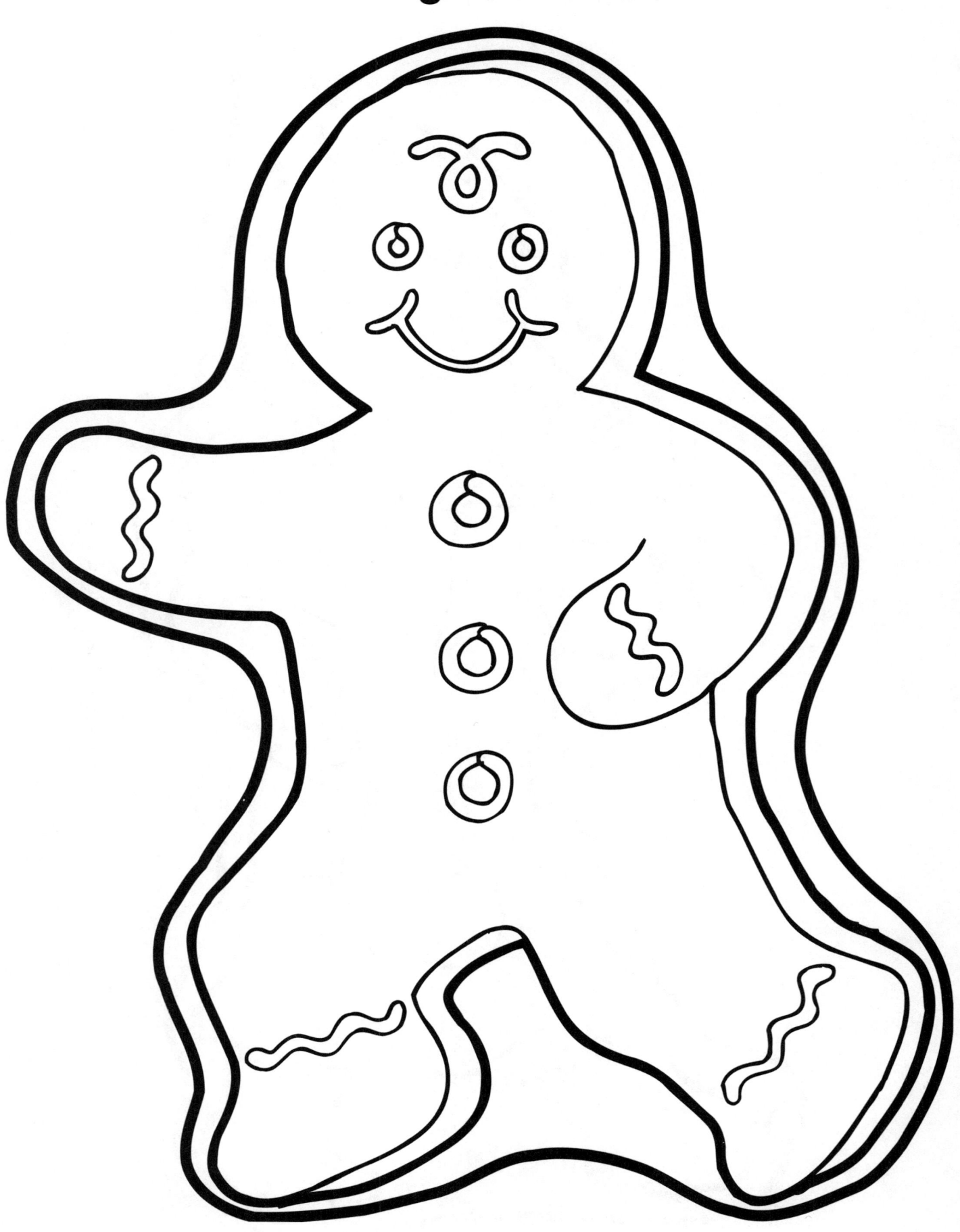

Humpty Dumpty

The King's Horses and the King's Men

© 1995 Monday Morning Books, Inc.

The Itsy Bitsy Spider

Jack and His Beanstalk

The Giant

Old King Cole

A King

The Little Mermaid

© 1995 Monday Morning Books, Inc.

Three Pairs of Mittens

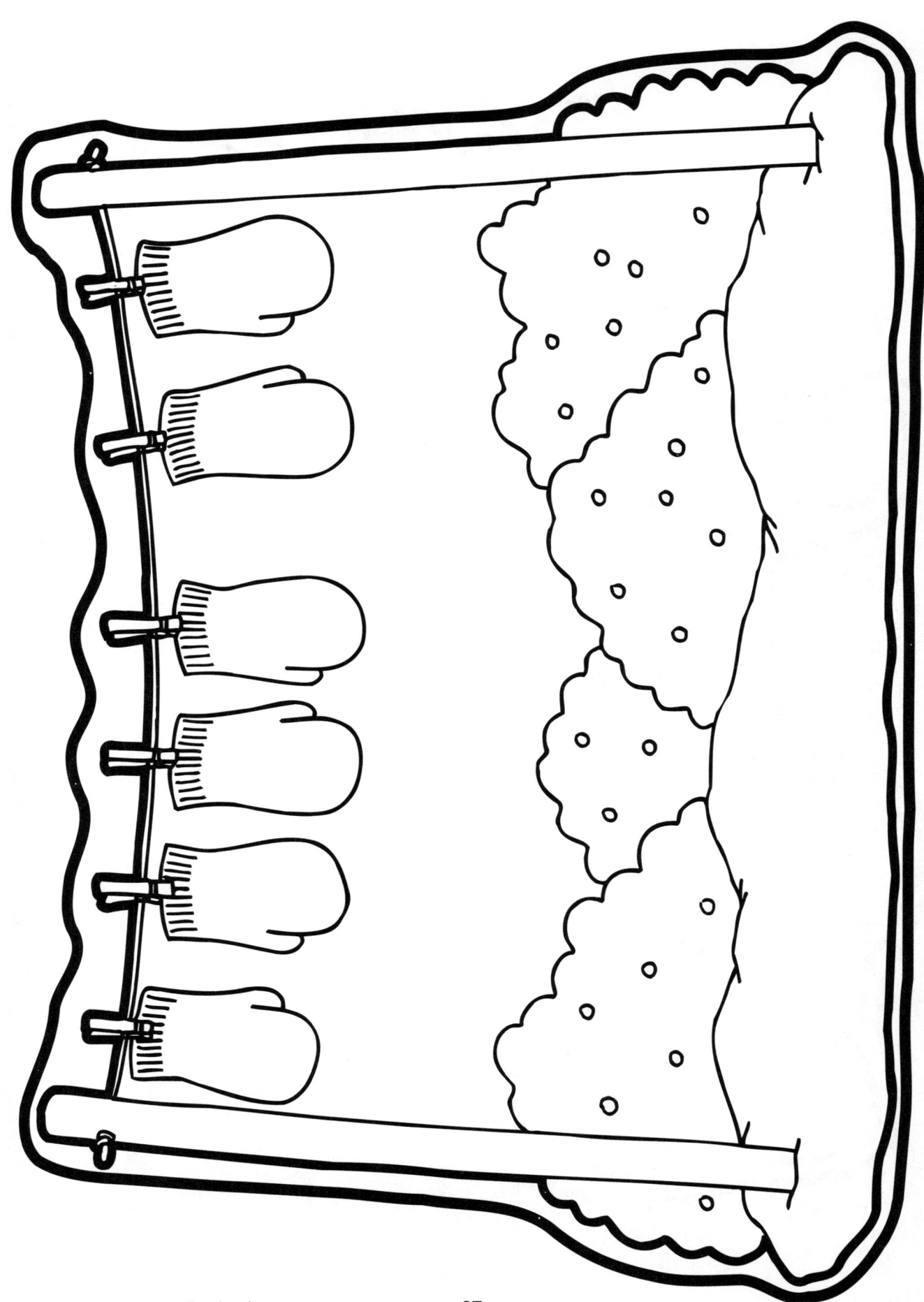

Three Little Kittens

Peter Pan

The "Clock-odile"

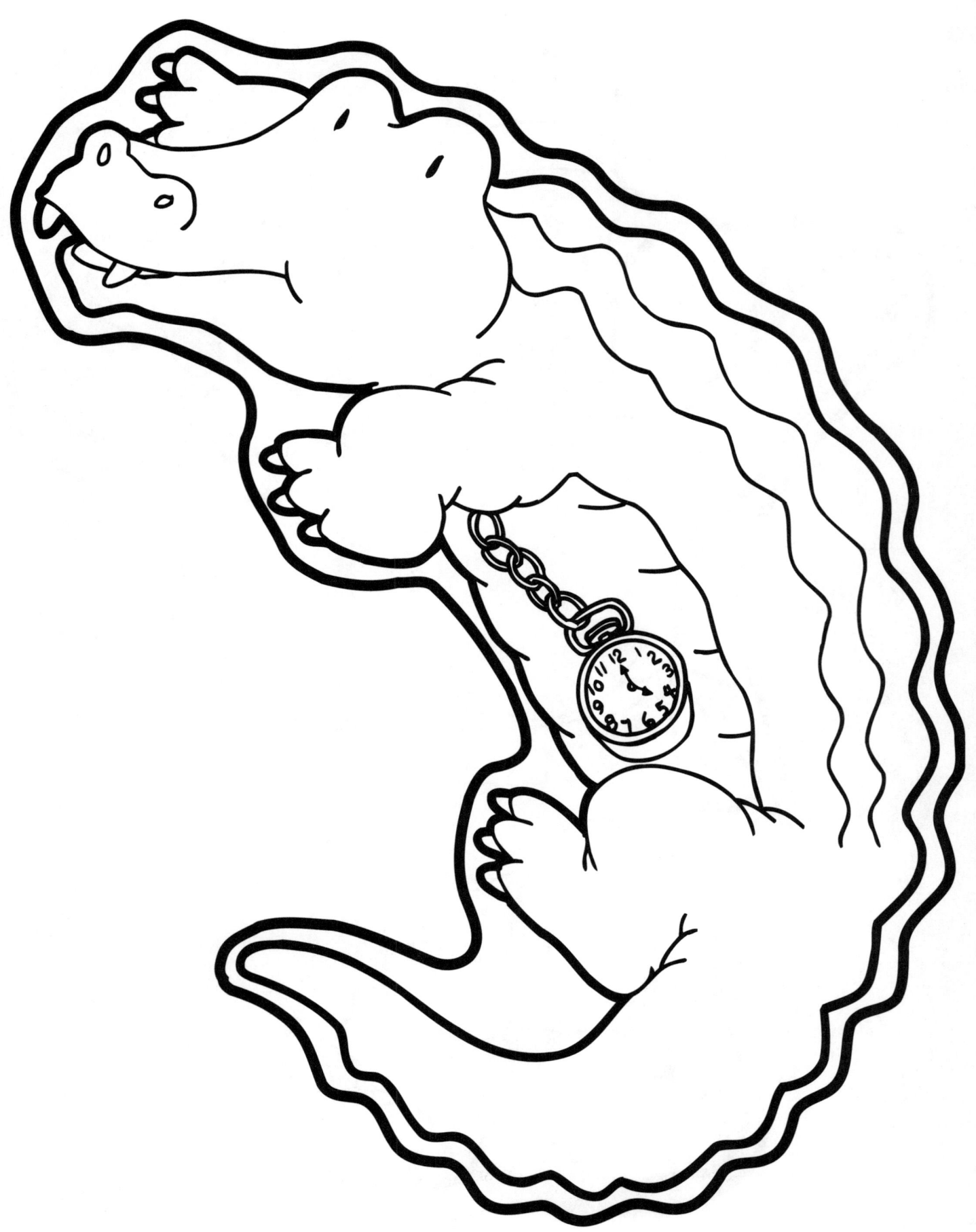

Captain Hook

An Old Lady

The Princess and the Pea

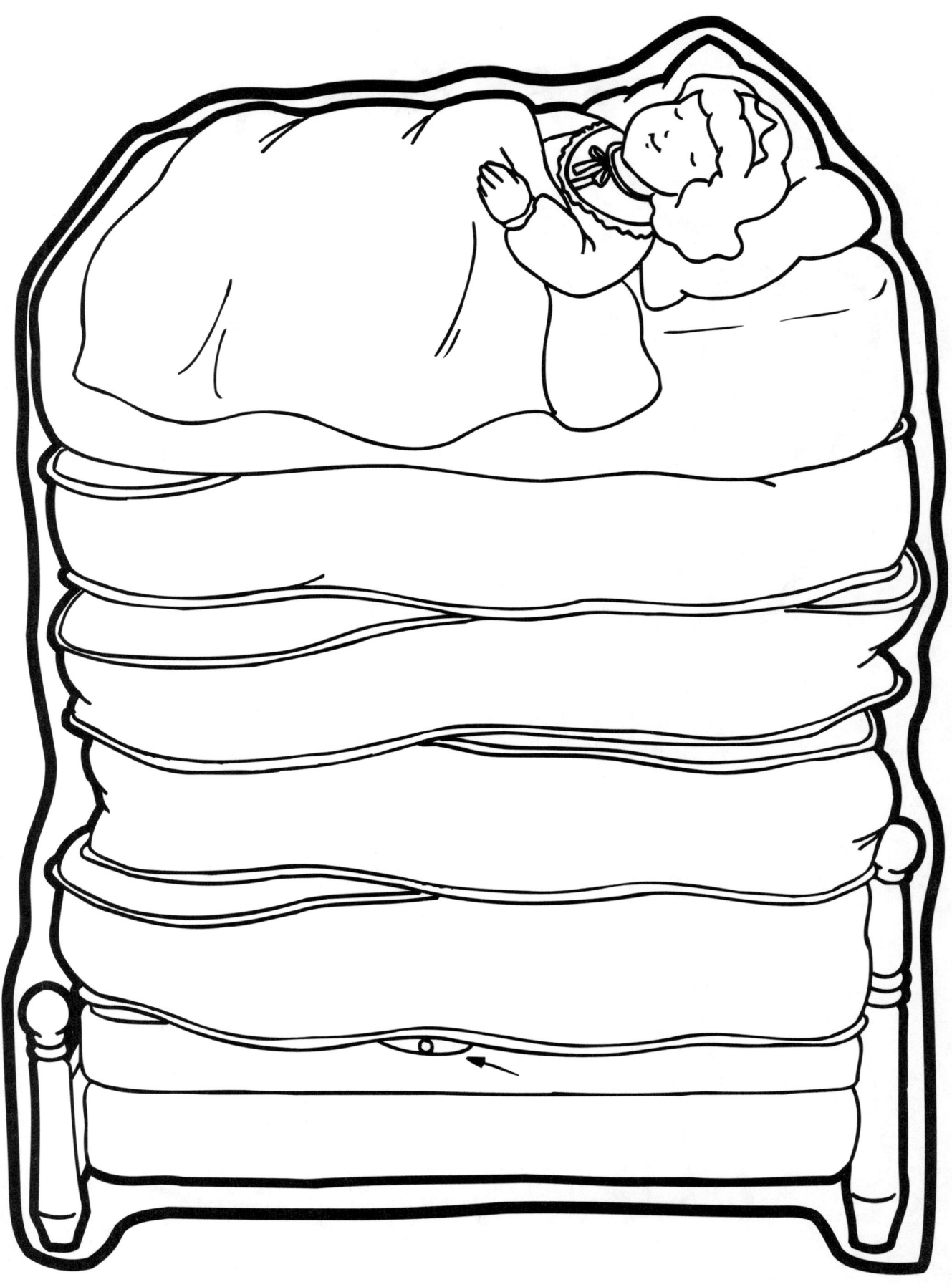

The Queen of Hearts

A Queen on a Throne

Rapunzel

A Blackbird Pie

A Maid

Thumbelina

Thumbelina and the Fairy Prince

The Ugly Duckling

The Swan

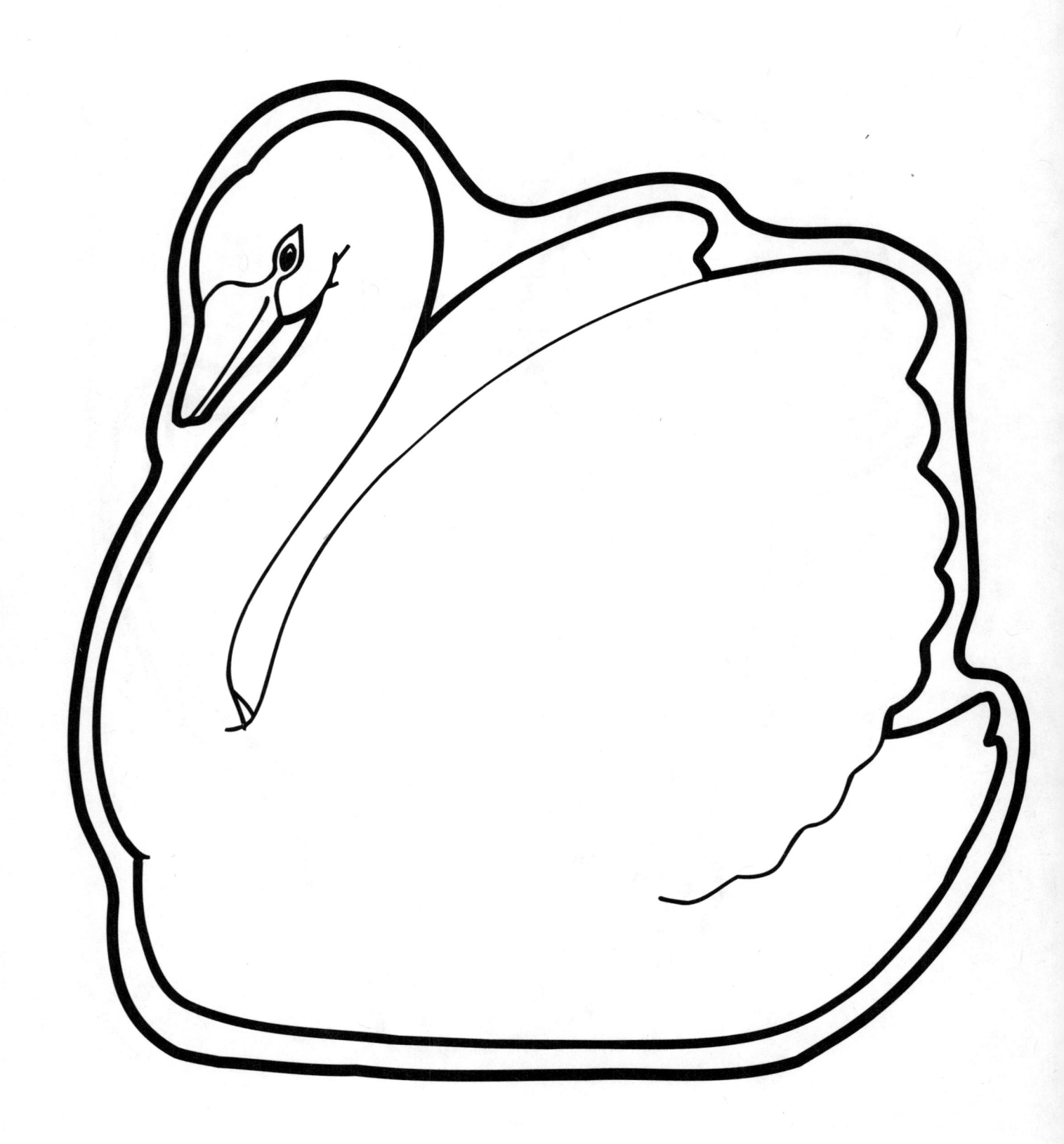

Rip Van Winkle

A Princess

A Flock of Wild Swans

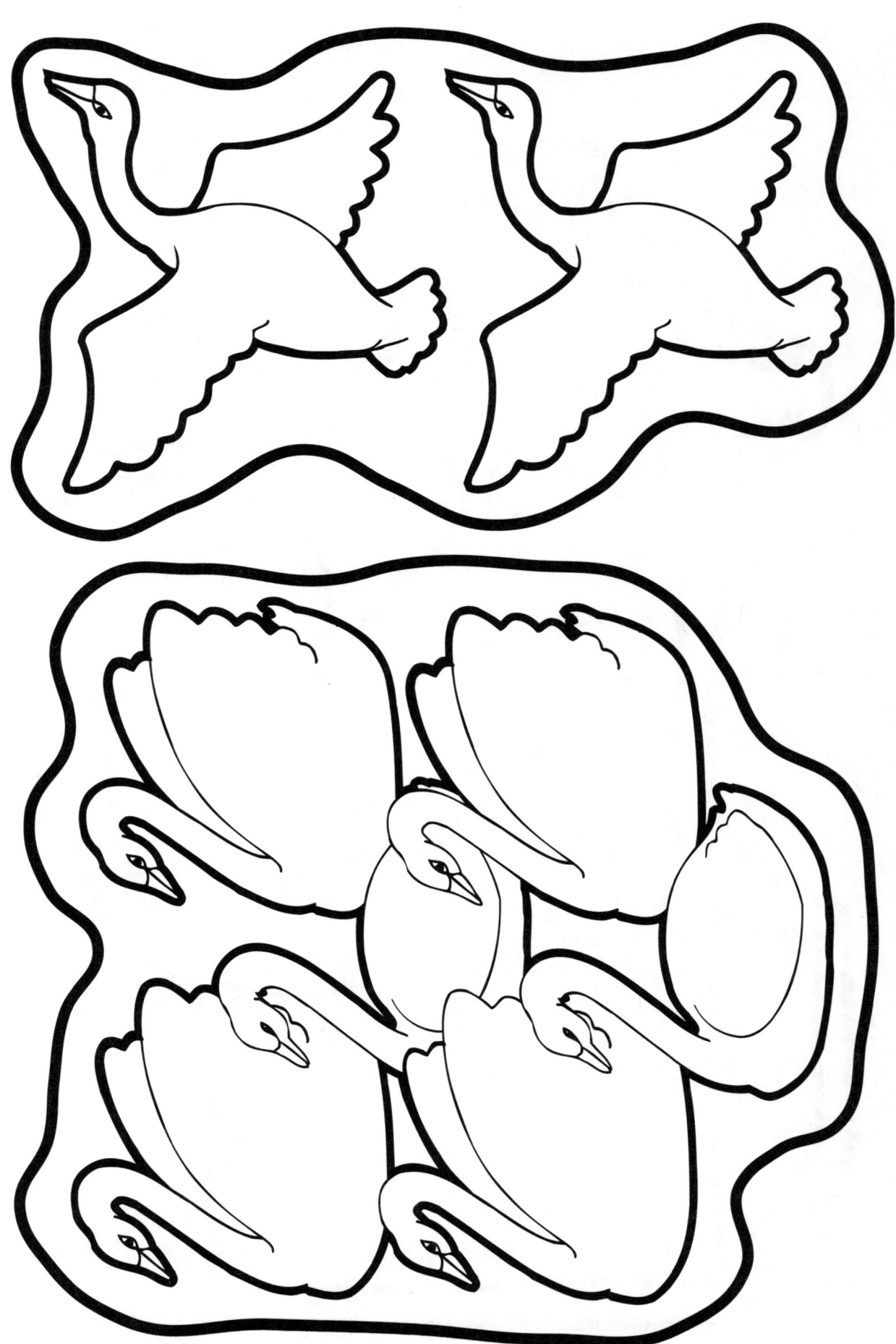

A Fox

Yetta the Trickster

© 1995 Monday Morning Books, Inc.

A Zebra in a Zoo

48

© 1995 Monday Morning Books, Inc.